Eben Newton Baldwin

The Engineer's Last Journey

And Other Poems

Eben Newton Baldwin

The Engineer's Last Journey
And Other Poems

ISBN/EAN: 9783744761109

Printed in Europe, USA, Canada, Australia, Japan

Cover: Foto ©Thomas Meinert / pixelio.de

More available books at **www.hansebooks.com**

THE

ENGINEER'S

LAST JOURNEY,

AND

OTHER POEMS.

— BY —

EBEN NEWTON BALDWIN.

THE

ENGINEER'S LAST JOURNEY,

AND

OTHER POEMS.

BY

EBEN NEWTON BALDWIN,

CLAYMONT, DELAWARE.

WILMINGTON, DEL.
FERRIS BROS., PRINTERS AND BOOK BINDERS.
1886.

This humble volume is fraternally dedicated to my brother
employees of the Philadelphia, Wilmington and
Baltimore Railroad Company.
June 1st, 1886.

CONTENTS.

THE

ENGINEER'S LAST JOURNEY,

AND OTHER POEMS.

THE ENGINEER'S LAST JOURNEY.

LIKE a Monarch in power, like a King on his throne,
Like an Emperor ruling his Empire—his own;
Like the fangs of the lightning, the might of the cloud
Is the strong Locomotive—so noble and proud.
While the hand of Jehovah commands the broad sky,
And grasps the proud helm when the storm rages high,
So the hand of proud man holds the lever of steam
As he sits at the helm of the engine—serene.

When the speed is the highest his glory is great,
His hopes are then brightest—he cannot be late.
Through the villas and farm-lands he dashes along,
And feels his great power, and whistles a song.
Though the midnight be gloomy, and murky the sky,
Though the storm be upon him, escapes not a sigh
As he fearlessly clings to the lever of power,
And blows the shrill whistle many times in an hour.

His motto is "Onward," he onward must go,
Sometimes like the lightning—sometimes rather slow ;
And sometimes he stops, but tarries not long,
For "Onward, still onward," is ever his song.
If you will but listen a moment to me,
I will tell you a story as sad as can be,—
The tale of an Engine, with *master* so true
That men stop and wonder ! no wonder they do.

" **77** " she wore on her breast as a sign—
For that was her number—her master's design.
Her arms were as mighty as cold steel could be,
Her weight many tons, in rich symmetry.
Her whistle was sharp and commanding as well;
But now to the story I promised to tell,
For never an engineer passes that spot,
But thinks the same thing might have been his own lot.

The Richmond Express, the great " Kennesaw route,"
Ran nightly along, with a pleasant salute,
And hardly a man or a boy in the town
But knew when she passed, and watched her go down.
On an evening, now passed, I remember it well,
When the darkness was dense, and no gleaming light fell,
Came the Richmond Express—like a bird did she fly—
Her sparks flew about her and lightened the sky.

The warnings came promptly as crossings drew near,
That all might be ready, that all might be clear ;
For woe to that object which dare to be found
On the track, it to atoms would surely be ground.
At the helm sat a man—the best work of God—
Who governed the speed of the train with a rod,
A lever so slender and yet with such power
As to bring in the train at the moment—the hour.

A youth only twenty was fireman that night,
And worked hard to keep his huge fire burning bright,
And thinking of when he should finish the "run,"
Vigilantly watching there—father and son.
Darby and Chester were left far behind,
And Linwood approached with a pleasant, fair wind.
Claymont drew near, and, sad to relate,
Father and son hastened on to their fate.

Onward, still onward, like a roe out of breath,
Little they knew the next station was DEATH.
Little they dreamed they were on the last "run,"
And that neither should enter the near Wilmington.
Crash! Crash! Crash! Great God! save the men,
Where have they landed? Oh! where, where or when?
Confusion, and terror, and darkness, and pain,
God save the fallen—restore them again!

God has now answered, the train is still there;
Never have any approached him in prayer
But what came the answer, came in some way,—
Of this rest assured, for surely you may.
Stillness now reigns, though the engine has gone.
Oh, what confusion I there look upon!
Father and son both found at their post,
Doing their best, though their lives they have lost.

Never did Spartans more courage display.
Spartans would die—likewise did not they?
Noble, brave men, you were faithful till death,
Faithful as long as the Lord gave you breath
When we are reading of Spartans of old
We shall remember your deeds to behold.
Ever when thinking of those we love most,
Remember the father and son at their post.

Bury them tenderly 'neath the green willow tree,
That the breezes may sing them a sweet lullaby,
Wafting o'er hill and dale, distant and near,
Deeds of the faithful ones slumbering here.
Cover their green graves in springtime with flowers,
Laden with perfume fresh plucked from the bowers.
Carve on the slab that you put near their grave :
" DIED WHILE IN DANGER, THEIR FELLOWS TO SAVE."

KILLED IN THE WRECK,

OR, WAITING FOR PAPA TO-NIGHT.

THE twilight shadows were falling
 As softly as white downy snow,
And the children their papa were calling,
 For papa was coming, you know.
In the morn, when the daylight was breaking,
 He had started to earn daily bread,
And long before children were waking
 He had left on the train, mamma said.

How he loved those bright, sunny faces,
 No one but a father can know ;
How he watched those developing graces,
 Is known to but few here below.
And that sweet companion—their mother—
 Was to him "all the world," I may say,
Far dearer than sister or brother,
 More charming than blossoms of May.

In the springtime of life, when the roses
　　Were fragrant with glistening dew,
He had met her—had offered her posies,
　　Like any gallant lover would do ;
And then at the most sacred altar,
　　When the murmur of voices was still,
In tones that knew not a falter,
　　He had whispered an earnest " I will."

Those hours were blissful and cheering,
　　And the time sped away fast and free ;
The ties of affection are endearing,
　　For God hath made the decree.
Well, time by-and-by brought sorrow,
　　And children soon played at the door,
But sunshine would come on the morrow
　　And all would seem bright as before.

They toiled and struggled together,
　　The vine clinging close to the oak,
Through all kinds of trouble and weather,
　　For God had placed on them the yoke ;
And papa worked hard, late and early,
　　And mamma was faithful and true,
She loved all her children most dearly,
　　God promised her grace to renew.

And now they played by the fireside,
　　Those children, with cheeks all aglow,
Of papa and mamma—their own pride,
　　For papa was coming, you know.
The playthings were hidden from sight,
　　Papà's slippers were placed in the glow
Of the red embers, cheery and bright,
　　For papa was coming, you know.

The hours passed wearily by,
  No footstep was heard at the gate,
And the baby for papa did cry,
  Because he was coming home late.
Through the darkness they eagerly peer,
  Down the street all covered with snow,
To watch for papa, so dear,
  For papa was coming, you know.

Oh children ! God pity you all !
  My heart aches to think your bright room
Must soon be changed to a pall,
  Must soon know sorrow and gloom.
Those innocent, pulsating hearts,
  So free from trouble and pain,
Must know the sad pangs of death darts,
  For papa shall come not again.

But, listen ! A footstep is heard ;
  Some one coming home in the dark.
Is it papa I hear, little bird ?
  What voice do I hear ?   Listen ! Hark !
A messenger sent down to say,
  That papa was on " *Thirty-nine.*"
An accident happened to-day,
  The word came over the line.

Oh, thunderbolt, long, fierce, and loud,
  From a sky so rosy and red !
Oh, man so noble and proud,
  Can it be that papa is dead ?
The messenger comes down once more,
  To say the saddest is true.
He gilded the tale that he bore,
  As any kind person would do.

And baby was sleeping so sweet,
  While the children were anxious to know
What tarried poor papa's tired feet,
  For papa was coming, you know.
Oh, God ! in humility bending,
  Thou alone canst these things understand ;
To those whose prayers are ascending,
  Speak peace, and strengthen each hand.

Thou, God, hast given and taken,
  Thy ways are past finding out,
But when, by-and-by, we awaken,
  Thy wisdom will banish our doubt.
Be a father to all the forsaken,
  And bless to that family this woe ;
Then when in thy presence they waken,
  They shall find darling papa, you know.

DID YOU EVER THINK?

YOU have heard the rain-drops beating
    On the roof when in your bed,
  Countless droppings oft repeating,
  Humming dirges for the dead.
You have heard the rain in torrents
  Pouring down on all below ;
Did you ever think what sent it,
  Whence it comes, where does it go ?

You have seen a field of flowers
  Nodding gently in the sun,
Seeming happy all the hours,
  Till the busy day was done ;

Did you ever stop to ponder
  At a sight so wondrous fair,
And to think each tiny leaflet
  Had some power for it to care ?

You have seen men who great glory
  Won upon life's battle field,
Who could tell you tale and story,
  How "*the right*" they would not yield ;
Did you ever think in silence
  Of the number and the style
Of the true, the great, the brave men,
  That are classed " *The rank and file* " ?

Men who, had they chance to show it,
  Would *exceed* the *best* now known,
Who could see a wrong, and know it
  Well as King on any throne,—
Men of souls, with hearts of kindness,
  Who could sway the rolling tide
Of mankind,—but hid in blindness,
  Thousands, millions such have died.

You have watched the mighty billow
  Of the ocean come and go,
Waving like a storm-tossed willow
  Troubled with a weight of woe ;
Did you ever think what power
  Caused such great, stupendous surge,
Year by year and hour by hour,
  Ceaseless chanting like a dirge ?

You have viewed the spangled wonders
  Of the heavens when all was clear,
You have heard the angry thunders
  Almost crash you when so near ;

Who so mighty lives to make it,
  Who with such a power or will,
When the storm is raging wildly,
  Sweetly whispers, " *Peace, be still* " ?

You have seen man's work and genius
  Send his thoughts to distant clime,
Under water, leagues and fathoms,
  While the clock could strike the time ;
Did you eyer stop in wonder,
  Stop, *stand still*, think of the law
That could govern such achievement
  Easy as you lift a straw ?

You have heard your own heart beating,
  Hour by hour and day by day,
Keeping time of life that's fleeting
  And that soon must pass away ;
What perpetuates such motion,
  What strange powers this great world move ?
I am lost in such an ocean—
  ' *Tis the ocean of God's love.*

"*I AM A JEALOUS GOD.*"

BOW not at any earthly shrine.
  The fullness of the earth is mine,
  The cattle on a thousand hills,
Ten thousand laughing free-born rills,
The treasures in the mighty deep,
The wealth down in the mines that sleep
Are mine—all mine.
Bow not at any earthly shrine.

The tenderest flowers that kiss the sun,
The grains of sand where children run,
The smallest leaves upon a tree
Are mine, and each is dear to me ;
The little ant that works all day,
That never stops to rest or play.
Is mine—entirely mine,
Bow not at any earthly shrine.

Bow not at any human shrine,
The human family is mine.   .
The loftiest thoughts that fill the brain
Are only from myself made plain ;
Man is my dearest work of all,
His intellect, so grand, so tall,
Is mine—all mine.
Bow not at any earthly shrine.

If men insist and disobey,
Then I will take their shrine away ;
" I am a jealous God," indeed.
Hear ye, and to my voice take heed :
Bow not at any earthly shrine,
I am the Lord, all power is mine,
Is mine—all mine.
Bow not at any earthly shrine.

NOW I LAY ME DOWN TO SLEEP.

THE storms of life are raging wild,
    And billows roll to press me down,
    But like a sweet and lovely child,
Rest is to me a golden crown.
My toil for one more day is done ;
    The quiet shadows softly creep.

My life is one day nearer run,
  And now I lay me down to sleep.

The weary day has been too long ;
  Its cares were very fierce and sore,
And though I tried to hold up strong,
  Now I am glad the day is o'er.
O angel, guard my humble bed ;
  Come near, and strictest vigil keep,
Preserve me, hand and heart and head,
  For now I lay me down to sleep.

The world I for a time forget,
  And soar to realms extremely fair ;
No trouble, sorrow, or regret
  Can ever dare to enter there.
In dreams of pleasure, half divine,
  I view great wonders, vast and deep ;
The genial *Sun* of *Love* is mine
  When in that wondrous land of sleep.

But, oh ! to wake, to realize
  This cold and cruel world again,
Were like the losing of some prize
  Which one expected to obtain.
But sometime—ah ! it may be soon,
  Kind friends may condescend to weep ;
I shall not heed midnight or noon,
  But all unconscious, sweetly sleep.

Seed-time and harvest will return ;
  Love shall endure and truth prevail ;
Passion the hearts of men still burn,
  And life go on, like some strange tale.
No sound shall interrupt my bliss,
  From these fond eyes no tears may weep ;
These lips, if any dare to kiss,
  I shall not heed, but sweetly sleep.

Cold, thankless world, so full of sin!
 Adieu; oh, let me take my rest
With sweet unconsciousness within,
 For I am weary and oppressed.
God hath provided me a rest;
 He would not have me always weep;
Oh! may his precious name be blest!
 Farewell—I lay me down to sleep.

THE WEEPING WILLOW.

EMBLEM of sorrow, tell me why
 Thy constant weeping, constant grief?
 Is it fear, a dread to die?
Does earth afford thee no relief?
Oh! tell me, drooping, heart-sick tree,
Tell me thy story, even me.

Then the Willow, as I calmly stood
 Rustled slightly, kissed by gentle wind,
And said, "Alone in all the wood
 I weep,—an emblem of mankind.
To thee the story I will tell;
But promise me to guard it well.

Then I said, "O Weeping Willow,
 I will keep thy story true,
And at night upon my pillow,
 I shall often think of you—
Think of you, at midnight weeping,
While the world is sweetly sleeping.

"Once in years, bright years gone by,
  I was happy, free, and gay,
All unclouded was my sky,
  And I often used to play;
But "—and here the Willow wept —
" From my youth I have not slept.

" Then there came an ardent lover,
  Who upon me lavished praise,
And his praises made life smoother,
  Through those happy, happy days,
And my heart with love was smitten,
Love—of which so much is written.

" I had promised when the flowers
  Bloomed again, the earth to cheer,
I would marry ' Ivy Bowers,'
  Marry him I loved so dear,
But alas! how vain is hope
With stern destiny to cope.

" I my garments had prepared,
  Robes of scolloped, tinted green,
And my prospect ' Ivy' shared,—
  Lovers true these things have seen,—
And the happy, happy day,
On time's pinions sped away.

" In the church-yard, near the door
  I stood waiting as there came
Crowds of people more and more,
  Soon, farewell my maiden name,
And I very nervous grew,
As most brides I think would do.

" Hark ! oh God ! I saw a coffin !
    Where was Ivy—Ivy dear ?
Not a smile was on their faces
    As they very close drew near,
And they raised the lid and said,
' This, your groom, you see is dead.'

" Oh, my bleeding heart that moment
    None shall ever, ever know ;
God forbid that any mortal
    Should be pained and frightened so,
And my bridal robes drooped down,
Drooped in sadness to the ground.

" Then they buried ' Ivy ' darling
    At my pure, white, slippered feet.
In the cold, damp ground they laid him—
    Laid my darling one so sweet.
And I stand—stand here and weep
O'er the spot where he doth sleep.

And at twilight every evening
    ' Ivy ' comes, his bride to greet.
Sweet communion then receiving,
    Lowly bending at my feet.
Oh, the rapture, oh, the bliss,
In his fond and loving kiss.

" I am dreaming—now awaking
    Stern reality to view,
Find my bleeding heart is breaking,
    That he comes, is too untrue,
Would that I could yet believe
He doth yet his bride receive.

" Do you wonder at my weeping,
    Now the story you have heard ?
Do you wonder at my keeping
    Strictest watch with beast and bird ?
Man—O man, wonder no more
That I weep forevermore.

" Every spring-time those green dresses
    Robe me as a waiting bride,
Diamond-jeweled leaves for tresses,
    With my white veil at my side.
Were I gone, my friends would miss me,
For the showers come and kiss me.

" All the livelong summer time,
    Sweet birds are my company,
And their songs of chant and rhyme
    Soothe my grief and comfort me.
But for ' Ivy ' I shall wait,
In the twilight, near the gate.

" And when autumn sere approaches,
    All my leaves like ermine turn,
When the frost on me encroaches
    Then my inward heart doth burn.
After that I shed my tresses,
Lovely leaves and bridal dresses.

"But each spring shall see me waiting
    In my lovely foliage green,
Lonely—sadly—half debating,
    Thinking of ' what might have been.'
' Ivy,' too, shall dwell the same,
At my feet, to bless my name."

Then I said, "O Weeping Willow,
  I shall not thy trust betray,
But at night upon my pillow,
  And all hours through the day,
I shall ever think of thee,
Thou hast been so kind to me.

"And when I shall leave this clime,
  When my life shall shortly fade,
They shall carry me and mine
  To recline beneath thy shade ;
Thou o'er me, then, too, can weep
As I lonely—sweetly sleep."

ALL WHOM I LOVE HAVE DIED.

A DREAM.

MOTHER dear was once my pride ;
  How steadfast is a mother's love ;
I said, "She ever shall abide,
  To make my pathway clear and smooth."
But as I hurried home, one day,
  Expecting words of kindest tone,
Death's dart had chanced to come that way,
  And pale in death she lay alone.

A father, manly, true, and brave,
  I then more closely, fondly loved ;
He would have died his boy to save.
  I had his loving kindness proved.
Alas! he, too, hath gone from me.
  One day he called me to his bed,
Kissing me fondly, lovingly,
  Said, "Son, I leave you," and was dead.

A sister fair I loved so well,
  A pearl of kindness in her found,
Her gentle chidings she would tell,
  And taught me virtue and renown.
When night was darkest, flashing wire
  Brought harsh and cruel words to me,
" Your sister is dead, and we desire
  You come—the funeral at three."

" A youthful brother, gay and proud,
  I now shall cherish evermore,
And him from all the throbbing crowd
  Shall be my heart's contented store."
Amid the roar of gun and fire,
  He left me for his country's sake ;
The battle-ground saw him expire
  Where sabres shine and cannons quake.

A fond companion and a wife
  God in his goodness made my own ;
She was myself, my very life,
  In purity and virtue shone.
She too hath gone and left me sad.
  My heart-strings now are almost riven,
But one thought cheers and makes me glad,
  And that is, she is safe in heaven.

I had a darling, prattling boy,
  His eyes were like ethereal blue,
His smiles, my sunshine and my joy,
  His innocence so pure and true.
One day his face had lost its glow,
  His eyes half closed, yet not a groan,
I placed my hand upon his brow—
  To heaven his little soul had flown.

Ah me ! for what have I to live,
　　Since all I ever loved hath died ?
Heart-broken I am left to grieve,
　　And never shall be pacified.
Never ? Ah yes ! A voice from heaven
　　I hear in loving accents call,
" They all are safe whom I had given
　　I have a purpose in it all."

*　　*　　*　　*

When I from dreamland came and found
　　My sorrow was not true nor real,
I, half bewildered, looked around ;
　　God knows how happy I did feel!
Then heavenward I cast mine eyes
　　To catch from God one gentle gleam,
There, looking steadfast to the skies,
　　Thanked God it all was but a dream.

"NOT NOW, BUT "BY-AND-BY."

AN infant, helpless, innocent, and sweet,
　　Lay calmly in his mother's arms so still,
Except the motion of his little feet
　　Which seemed to move about at will.
I said, " Kind woman, what do you expect
　　Of such a little mite—but fret and cry ?"
She said, " Young man, reflect, reflect, reflect,
　　What he may be—in some sweet by-and-by.

A barefoot boy, along the brook at play,
　　With sun-burnt hands and dirty face,
No trouble written on his brow,—that day
　　He thought of nothing save that pretty place.

I said, " My son, what do you really think
  Will be your lot in life ?"   Then with a sigh
He said, " I live to play—to eat, to sleep,
  And be a man—in some sweet by-and-by."

A youth of twenty next came walking down,
  And his fair cheeks with perfect health did
      glow ;
He was indeed the pride of all the town ;
  His voice was charming, and his step not slow.
I said, " Young man, how s it now with thee ?
  What thy ambition, aspiration high ?"
He answered, looking wonderingly at me,
  " I hope for happiness, some time, by-and-by."

Upon his door-step sat a man at rest,
  After the weary labor of the day,
Two children near—another close he prest,
  And this is what I heard him say ;
" My darling wife, we shall be happy soon,
  May these our darling children never cry,
This trouble shall be gone like yonder moon.
  For us comes comfort in the by-and-by."

I turned and onward plod my way,
  But standing near my path I saw a bending
      form,
Gray beard and hair—yea, very, very gray,
  And marks of life's most careworn storm.
" Dear father," said I, " how is it, I pray ?
  What is the latest watchword from on high ?
He answered, " Keep the narrow, narrow way,
  And trust ; there's resting by-and-by."

An old, old man, upon his daughter's knee
  Lay helpless—even like the little child ;
His weary eyes long had ceased to see,
  And very faint his voice—and very mild.
I said, " Kind father, what was life to thee ?
  Why moan—and why thy long-drawn sigh ?"
He said, " Beyond is happiness for me,
  And peace and joy awaits me, by-and-by."

Into the church they bore the white-haired man,
  Life from its worn-out shell had fled at last,
From weeping eyes the sad tears freely ran,
  To think the final end had come at last.
A solemn hymn was sung in solemn strain,
  And many a heartfelt, weary sigh
Went up, as over and again—again—
  They sang, "There's resting by-and-by."

Then speaking to myself, I said, "Young man,
  This is thy consummation and thy end ;
Thy life is like a narrow shadow span,
  Uncertain, but on death thou may'st depend."
Sorrowful at heart and bowed down with grief,
  Miserable I felt, for this I won't deny,
But oh ! I found such calm relief
  In thinking of that happy by-and-by.

The heart of man, so dwarfed, cannot conceive
  What joy awaits him at the Master's call;
But oh ! I realize and firmly do believe,
  One hour in heaven will repay it all.
High heaven, teach us with toil to strive and live
  So we may never, never fear to die—
Ourselves to thee in sweet humility to give,
  And wait thy pleasure to us—by-and-by.

THE HUNGRY EARTH.

"BRING me your dead—bring them along ;
   I have swallowed millions before ;
This is forever and ever my song,
  Bring me your dead evermore.
I swallowed old patriarchs and thousands untold,
  All drowned by the flood were sweet food to me,
I hunger and thirst for the young and the old,
  And never shall cease, till man cease to be.

" Bring me your dead; like a ravenous beast,
  I gobble them down at a mouthful or less,
Dead men and dead women are ever my feast,
  Regardless of beauty, of fashion or dress.
Infants are food for me—morsels so sweet
  That Jupiter might envy my place in the air,
I nothing care for but to eat, eat, eat
  Mankind, overtaken by death and despair."

Oh ! cruel Earth, why will you take
  My darlings from my side ?
My bleeding heart, why will you break,
  And not be satisfied ?
Yea, no ! For I myself must come
  To be thy food ere long, I know,—
Must in thy bosom find that home
  Destined to mortals here below.

This hand which moves this weeping quill,
  So active and so wondrous wrought,
Soon in thy bosom calm and still,
  Shall rest – life's battle having fought.
This sparkling eye, this beaming face,
  This throbbing heart, this quivering brain,
Alike shall follow in the race,
  And take their place in death's strong chain.

But while I on this picture dwell,
  And ponder o'er this ghastly sight,
A voice in whispers come to tell,
  And urge me, " Ever do the right."
For while this body shall decay
  This spirit must forever live ;
Christ hath himself prepared the way,
  And doth his sweet salvation give.

A throne of splendor, white as snow,
  Where angels ever sweetly sing
Awaits the spirit that below
  Gives sweet obedience to its King.
Since glory shall our portion be,
  Old Earth, yawn on ! we fear no more.
We shall the King of glory see,
  While surges swell from shore to shore.

A VISIT HOME.

I'VE been back to Harford, boys,
    And spent the livelong day
  Amid the scenes where youthful joys
    Once quickly sped away ;
The white-haired boys that I left
  Have grown to big stout men ;
And some of loved ones are bereft,
  Who gave much promise then.

The old school house is just the same
  As when we went to school ;
The benches where we cut our name—
  Where birch rods used to rule ;

But we were bad as boys are
    When at that certain age ;
And then the girls were very fair—
    You know they were the rage.

I now must tell you that the hand
    That flogged us time again,
Is resting in a better land
    From earth's turmoil and pain.
To Woodbury he moved away,
    To make a change, you know ;
He died ! poor " Jimmy Loflin " gray !
    Whose hair was white as snow.

Ah, few were souls more honest, boys,
    Than our dear white-haired sire,
But now he perfect bliss enjoys,
    'Twas long his chief desire.
And I must tell you while I think,
    The wood is cleared away,
The spring that furnished us with drink,
    Seems to have gone astray.

For not a tree is near it now,
    But corn is growing high,
And it has known the axe and plow,
    It almost made me cry !
As I was walking down the lane,
    Where oft we played of old,
I wished I were a boy again,
    And not my birth-right sold.

The cherry trees we used to climb
    Are blighted with decay ;
I used to call the large one mine,
    In that bright happy day.
You scarcely now would know the place,
    A'down by Hoofman's mill,

The banks are broken on the race,
　　The busy hum is still.

We used to know each face around
　　Those places long ago,
But strangers' voices are the sound
　　You hear where'er you go.
Upon a thriving old beech tree
　　I cut my sweet heart's name ;
No traces of the tree I see,
　　Since those new-comers came.

In life's great drama we must stand,
　　And act our special part,
Whether our own or foreign land,
　　Must show a loyal heart.
The little moss-roofed church is still,
　　As lonely as before.
At eve the saddened whip-poor-will
　　Sings to it o'er and o'er.

The graveyard slabs have thicker grown,
　　Scattered on every hand.
The weeping grass has not been mown,
　　Lonely it seems to stand.
The " Mud-town branch " looks very small,
　　But I would rather say
'Tis just because we, one and all,
　　Have seen old Ocean gray.

The sun-fish and the speckled trout
　　Grew fewer, year by year ;
Our pin hooks used to pull them out,
　　And it was sport most dear.
With wrapping twine and bent pin hooks,
　　We wandered in the sun
Along the stream, in shady nooks,
　　To have our boyish fun.

My heart was very, very sad,
  In leaving *that loved spot*,
For as a barefoot school-boy lad
  I vowed, " *Forget thee not.*"
And ever to that promise true,
  Wherever I may be,
My utmost power exert—I'll do ;
  " Still I'll remember thee."

Where are the many little boys,
  Who fondly used to play ?
Earth's glittering show a part employs,
  And part have passed away,
And when my time shall roll around
  And fade all earthly joy,
Take me where wild-wood's pleasant sound,
  First knew me—*as a boy.*

. THE WEDDING.

H, come to the wildwood, hasten away,
  The maple and willow were married to-day ;
  The willow, so modest, is weeping for joy,
The maple is blushing like a bashful school-boy.

All winter in silence together they stood,
But they mated and loved in the happy wild-wood,
They plighted their troth, so the little birds say,
The maple and willow were married to-day.

AUTUMN.

BEAUTIFUL maiden with golden hair,
Your voice is sweet, your face is fair ;
You smile upon the earth again,
And color your cheeks with luscious stain.

Your footsteps over hill and vale
Are known by the beautiful crimson trail ;
A stillness reigns,—a quiet hush,
That makes the ivy sumac blush.

Thy lover, old Winter, will wed thee soon,
For he whispers love as he views the moon,
His rugged arm shall clasp thy form
With the warmth of love, in the furious storm.

Thy children Spring and Summer shall be,
As beautiful as sisters who well agree,
I love thee, sweet maiden with golden hair,
For thy musical voice, and thy form so fair.

A RETROSPECT.

MEMORY, swing back again thy golden-tasseled door,
Reveal the many wonders within thy boundless store,
Show me my happy childhood, its sunshine and flowers,
The dear old home, I love it, bring back those happy hours.
As I sit alone at midnight,
By the dim and cheerless firelight,
When the world is sweetly sleeping,
And my eyes grow dim with weeping,
Then memory of childhood
When I wandered in the wildwood
Comes to cheer me, comes to bless,
With its soothing blessedness.

It shows the country school-house, with the children at play,
I see the fragrant meadows, and almost smell the hay ;
The blossoms in the orchard, the bride-dressed cherry tree,
The angel of sweet memory wafts them all back to me.
    I wander by the brookside ;
    Nude children in the brook glide
    From the overhanging limb,
    As they try to learn to swim.
    I hear the teacher's praises,
    Or I gathered ox-eyed daisies ;
    In the water at the spring,
    My image self I fling.

Oh, the sweet and happy faces I see in memory's glass,
Kaleidoscopic lenses, as one by one they pass.
Alas ! 'tis all a shadow, the substance long hath fled,
And those dear and smiling faces are silent with the dead.
    But I know they are at home
    No more therefrom to roam, ·
    Safe beyond the crystal tide
    With the Savior glorified.
    Fall gently, gentle rain,
    For we shall meet again
    On that bright and happy shore
    Where farewells are said no more.

AN EARLY RAMBLE.

COME ramble an hour with me,
    To see the first dawn of the light.
  The bird is awake in the tree,
    With " Farewell " to the vanishing night.
A silence, a stillness supreme,
    Seems to permeate everywhere,
As if in a half-waking dream,
    Or the silence of unspeakable prayer.

Behold the first streaks of the sun !
　The footprints of angels they seem ;
Wherever an angel hath run,
　The impress of golden sunbeam.
Yon star grows gradually dim,
　Though brightly and lovely it shone,
Its face turns sweetly to Him
　Who all of its secrets hath known.

The wild-rose is blushing with joy ;
　The golden-rod catches the light ;
The little stream laughs like a boy,
　When filled with some pleasing delight.
The bridal elder-blossom seems faint
　As it looks in the water below,
To see the the wild rose with its paint,
　And its own cheeks whiter than snow.

But hark to the dense leafy wood !
　What a minstrelsy filleth the air !
'Tis the sweetness of Birdie-bard-hood
　With a surplus of joy to spare.
'Tis delightful at breaking of day
　To ramble alone in the fields,
To hear what the little birds say,
　To see what kind nature yields.

Follow the stream to the glen,
　And leisurely walk in the grove,
For God is out walking then,
　And he whispers of infinite love.
For mankind worry and fret,
　And knit a brow dark as the night ;
But trust him, and do not forget
　Whatever he doeth is right.

GRANDMA'S LAMENT.

THE world is not the same old world
  Of seventy years ago,
For everything seems changed about,
And things have altered so.
Where is the humming spinning-wheel,
  The homespun mitts and socks ?
They say the poor man is outdone
  By the fellow with the " rocks."

"The rocks"—well, sakes alive, indeed,
  What thing is meant by that ?
For on the old farm where I lived
  We had 'em round and flat.
"Means money!"—why not say so, then ?
  I can't tell what you mean,
For half you say is Dutch to me—
  Something I never seen.

If little Jane is off for school,
  With books she must devour,
She waves her hand to me and says,
  "I'm off, so *au revoir.*"
The boys with all their books in hand,
  While looking for a hat,
Keep mumbling o'er and o'er again,
  "Amo, amas, amat."

And Will has bought a new machine,
  He rides up in the air ;
He took a "header" t'other day,
  And his cheeks are not so fair.
Instead of ox-carts, like we had,
  And plain and simple dress,
On the "elevated road" they gad,
  Or the "limited express."

'Tis very late when John comes in ;
   He ought to come home sooner.
He shouts "Oh, I have got the tin,
   And I want another 'schooner.'"
"A schooner, John!" says I to him,
   " To the sea will you be gone ?"
"Oh mother, hush, you make me tired,
   You never can 'catch on.' "

" Catch on to what ?   Who ever heard
   Such nonsense from a man ?
But when I say a word, they say,
   " We've got you in a pan."
And if I still remonstrate,
   And tell them it is rude,
They strut away like a peacock with
   " Oh, I'm a dandy dude."

Yes, everything is changed about,
   And the dear old Bible, too ;
I love the dear old comforter,
   But now they have the new.
It used to have a burning hell
   For the wicked without soul,
But they have stricken the hot word out,
   And made it read "Sheol."

Alas ! and I am changed, too,
   And my wrinkles hasten fast ;
But God will make my garments new,
   And take me home at last.
His love and mercy cannot change,
   For they are firm and true,   ˙
And his pardon for myself I ask,
   And his loving grace for you.

THE HERO SLEEPS.

HE sleeps! He sleeps! the nation's dead!
   No more shall sorrow cloud his brow,
   The thunders roll above his head,
The lightnings paint the heavens red ;
   No storms disturb his slumber now.

The nation's pride belongs to fame,
   He sleeps the peaceful sleep of death,
But those unborn shall praise his name,
His glory, like a seething flame
   Shall live while thrones are crushed beneath.

The bugle blast, the muffled drum,
   The human trail of crimson gore,
Are nought to him, his ear is dumb;
They startle not,—no more benumb,
   The tumult of his life is o'er.

Oh, why should mortal man be proud ?
   For glory leads but to the grave !
The king, the multitude, the crowd,
In Mother Earth shall find a shroud,
   Or sink beneath the blue sea wave.

But fame, immortal fame shall live,
   While mortal man can lisp a prayer,
For God immortal fame doth give ;
This truth into the heart receive,
   Immortal fame is rare.

Sleep on, O hero ! sleep in peace,
   While all the nation bows in woe,
May bickerings of nations cease,
Thy caution was, "Let us have peace."
   Sweet be thy *peace* where roses blow.

THE DEATH OF MY LITTLE FRIEND.

THE Master hath need of such for his King-
dom.   The little darling is safe on the
bosom of that dear lover of little children.
Many children are his, and one by one he gathers
them home ;

Gently folds them to his bosom,
  Kindly keeps them safely there,
Safely from all this world of sorrow,
  Safe from every blighting care.
Oh, he loves them most sincerely,
  Better than an earthly love,
And he folds them to his bosom,
  Where the flowers bloom above.

We shall meet our little children
  When the pearly gates we see.
What a welcome they will give us,
  What a meeting it will be !
Savior, safely keep them for us,
  Tenderly within the fold,
Give us grace to bear the burden,
  Bring us to the streets of gold.

THE WOODBINE.

A HONEYSUCKLE vine climbs up our cottage door,
  And throws it lovely shadows upon our humble floor,
  And it casts its sweetest perfume about our humble home,
Its little tendrils are ever wont to roam.

Beneath its lovely shadows I have sat me down to think,
And from its simple flowers some pleasures tried to drink,
And oh, the very sweetest thoughts are ever, ever mine,
As I sit in humble silence 'neath that honeysuckle vine.

Two white-haired little boys prattle upon the floor,
And sing and crow and hollow, by the honeysuckle door.
A humming-bird comes culling from every little flower,
And thus I while away, at times, a happy, happy hour.

O heart, be though content, and no more fret nor pine,
For there is pleasure, surely, 'neath the honeysuckle vine,
With humming-birds and children, and music in the air,
I could not wish a home more beautiful and fair.

THE FIRST SNOW.

IT snows as I sit at my window
  And enjoy the beautiful sight,
The snow-birds in soft downy garments
  Seem perfectly crazed with delight.
Softly and noiseless it falleth,
  White, pure, and tranquil and sweet,
Like unto silence that's golden,
  Like to the angel's soft feet.

Why o'er my heart steals a sadness,
  A shadow cast over my soul ?
The snow once filled me with gladness,
  And seemed but the height of my goal.
The snow is the same, I am certain,
  As pure and as white as before,
With its rich and lace-like curtain
  For window or transom or door.

The snow-birds are just as pretty
  As when I was a boy,
And I wonder why they don't give me
  The same happy pleasure and joy.
The cedars are festooned in beauty,
  The hemlocks wear robes like a bride,
But my heart grows weary in thinking
  Of my *dear little boy*, who died.

His sweet sunny face comes before me
  As I look at the beautiful snow,
And I think how he loved its beauty
  Only a very short year ago.
I remember, too, my father,
  And I think of the dear long ago
When he took us children sleighing,
  Each season, on the very first snow.

Dear loved one, my heart is weary,
  As I look at the snowing to-day,
And my soul is heavy and dreary
  And joy has hastened away.
Under the snow they are sleeping,
  Sweet be their rest below,
Fall lightly while I am weeping,
  Fall gently, beautiful snow.

But while their bodies are buried
  Under the beautiful snow,
Their souls are sweetly resting
  Where chilling winds cannot blow.
Safely they rest with the Savior,
  No sorrow, no death shall they know,
And their garments are whiter, I'm certain,
  Than the pure and beautiful snow.

OUR LITTLE BABE THAT DIED.

SWEET, innocent rosebud, slumber away;
  Rest gently, nor wake to the trouble of day.
  The Savior, who gave, hath taken his own,
To abide in his bosom, on his heavenly throne.
No blasts of a lifetime can mar thy sweet face,
Nor sorrow nor trouble thy charms shall erase.

No death in that city to which thou hast flown,
The Savior hath claimed thee, his darling, his own.

Our hearts are saddened, and great is the pain
When we think we shall never see thee again,
But we know thou art safe in the glorious fold,
Where the walls are of jasper, the streets of pure gold.
Wherefore so soon hast thou taken thy flight,
Our darling, our hope, our pride, our delight?
Is earth too dreary, too cold, too severe,
For our little rosebud, so precious, so dear?

Ah! God and his ways are wondrous indeed.
To search him were vain, man cannot succeed;
But simply to trust him, in faith, full and free,
Leads man from himself, and nearer to thee.
Sweet, innocent rosebud, slumber away,
Nor wake to the sorrow and care of the day.
Safe, safe in the arms of the Savior recline,
For the bliss and the joy of heaven is thine.

VERNON.

DIED AT SUNSET.

JUST as the twilight gathered,
        Over hill and vale,
        The angels called our darling,
    His life was a finished tale.
And his little snow-white fingers
    Were peacefully at rest,
For his dimpled hands we folded
    Upon his peaceful breast.

Sad is our home, sweet darling,
    We loved our boy so well.
Oh! the love we bore our loved one
    We cannot begin to tell;

And our hearts with pain are riven,
  And sorrow clouds our brow,
For our darling beautiful boy
  Is not with us now.

But safe in the arms of Jesus
  His innocent soul must be,
For the request of the Savior was truly,
  Let the little ones come unto me ;
And though he slay, we will trust him.
  His precious name we'll adore,
Till we meet our boy angel
  On the strand of the beautiful shore.

CLYDE HILL, CLAYMONT.

WHERE will you find a spot more fair,
  With finer view, or purer air ?
    The sweet and balmy breath of spring,
Back from the south-land its flowers bring ;
The morning sun, with its wealth of gold,
Brings precious visions of wealth untold.

Gaze with me on yon glimmering stream ;
The beautiful river, like a fairy dream,
Lies tranquil, as in sweet repose,
While onward, forever onward it flows,
The carnal heart, and the carnal will
Are thus — till a voice says, " Peace, be still."

See yon ship, with its snowy sail,
Like a pale, winged bird, so tender and frail ;
From what port, bound to what haven,—where ?
What precious burden does it bear ?
No one can tell ; but onward it flies,
Over beautiful waters, under beautiful skies.

The land of the melon, on the other side,
Will soon be robed like a blushing bride,
And the river will kiss her ruby lips,
And blossoms adorn her, and lady " whips."
Where the Indian kissed his wife and child,
Loves soothes the pale-face, and makes him mild.

The farmer slowly plows the field,
And trusts to heaven a generous yield,
He sows the wheat and plants the corn,
And is glad when he hears the dinner-horn.
As he homeward starts he is filled with bliss,
For his wife and child await his kiss.

The cattle graze in quiet peace,
In a dozen fields they take their ease ;
The tender grass is a continual feast
To the dumb, but useful, noble beast.
Oh, God ! thy gifts are all divine,
And the cattle on a thousand hills are thine.

ADIEU.

FAREWELL, our beautiful boy,
    With angels thou dost dwell,
  But the sadness of our hearts
    We cannot begin to tell.
The Savior needed the flower,
    To plant in his garden up there,
He selects the loveliest buds
    For the kingdom so golden and fair.

We miss our beautiful boy,
    Our home seems lonely and sad ;
We miss his innocent smile,
    His laugh when merry and glad.

But we know he is safe in the fold
Of the Savior in Heaven so free,
Who said when on earth to mankind,
" Let the little ones come unto me."

— - —— —————

TWENTY-FIVE.

A M I half through my journey up to the golden gate,
Where loved ones gone before me in sweet contentment
wait ?
My life is flowing onward, whether I fail or thrive,
For in the near September I shall be twenty-five.

It does not seem so very long, when I was but a boy,
As my two little darlings now, who are my pride and joy ;
But when I come to count it up—alas ! I find it true,
And yet so much have I to learn, this life seems yet but new.

Troubles have come, even to me, but yet I can't complain,
For they must come at every step, and come and come again ;
But I have found a fountain pure to wash them all away,
And though sometimes the night be dark, I see the peep of day.

Companion, friend, whoe'er you are, who with me stem the flood,
I freely tell you I have found "a fountain filled with blood."
And oh, the very darkest night is transformed into day,
To those who, "plunged beneath that flood, wash all their sins
away."

Think of a hundred years to come, one moment look away,
Where will you be — where will I be, a hundred years to-day ?
Now where is haughtiness and pride ? Oh ! can they still remain,
Or does the very thought of death cause agony and pain ?

That we are passing swift away, no one can well deny.
Shall we sink down in deep despair, or soar beyond the sky ?
We cannot save ourselves, you know, of that we all are sure,
But there's a ransom for us, if we to the end endure.

O mighty Father, pity all, down in this vale below ;
If thou from us but hide thy face, oh whither shall we go ?
Earth hath no resting-place for our poor weary feet,
Hence we would very humbly bow down at thy mercy-seat.

Help me to keep the prize in view — a crown of gold the best —
When I shall bathe my weary soul in seas of heavenly rest.
There not a wave of trouble rolls, nor roaring tempest drive,
What need I care if fifty come, or only twenty-five.

A STARRY NIGHT.

UPON a still, calm night, when all the world doth rest,
I looked up to a sight that fills my throbbing breast,
That fills me as I see, in such enormity,
The wondrous firmament's whispered glory !
Oh, could I pierce beyond this vale of deep despond,
What visions there would greet me — what a story
Could I then tell my fellows — bound for vast Eternity.

But I am lost — to count the cost ;— to pierce the sky,
And there behold the lever which moves such wondrous beauty,
The abyss of immensity is the cavern into which I fall.
Oh ! I am lost ! — am swallowed up — reason and all,
Am taught how weak, how ignorant, and how blind
Is human understanding — and I find
Low down,— deep, deeper still, I fall.

Behind the scene if I could look — then I could write book
    upon book,
But that were not to be,— mortal could never look and live.
The bright and starry sky shelters me like a tent,
My efforts all are vain to rest and be content.
The Bible makes it plain. Oh, we shall live again
Beyond the stars,— those lovely gems on which we look,—
Shall rest in perfect peace and love,— forever there remain.

GOLDEN AUTUMN.

FADING glory, sun-kissed leaves,
    Painted by Artist from on high.
    O heavy-laden golden sheaves !
O lovely tinted autumn sky !
O footprints left by hoary frost,
    Which steals so noiseless while we sleep.
In meditation I am lost ;
    I humbly bow to thee — and weep.

I trace the *Master Artist's* hand
    O'er every hill, o'er every vale.
The colors blend at his command ;
    O'er every wild-wood in the dale
The hawthorn blushes at his touch ;
    The crimson sumac — poison vine —
To posies turn, and stand as such
    To speak the Master's fame divine.

The maple to the breezes nod,
    The chestnut bristles with its yield,
Wild calias and the golden-rod
    Make one grand bouquet of the field.

Bright ermine apples strew the ground,
    And few are left upon the trees;
The plum and apricot abound,
    Guarded by hungry honey-bees.

The meadow lark still soars on high
    With golden plumage — mellow song,
The unhusked corn is crisp and dry,
    The darkened shadows now are long;
Tomatoes glisten in the sun
    In beauty like some rosy maid;
The long, hot sultry days are done,
    And we approach old winter's shade.

The summer birds away have flown
    To sunny lands where spring abides;
Their little beauties now are grown,
    They, too, have gone — and all besides.
The last rays of yon sinking sun
    Shed forth a halo lovelier far,
Proclaiming one more day is done,
    And bows to yon bright evening star.

My fellow-traveller to the grave,
    May thy declining autumn be
As peaceful as the gentle wave
    Of some calm, smooth, untroubled sea.
Oh, may thy autumn waft to thee
    Sweet melody, in fullest strain,
Thy couch a bed of roses be,
    Thy life go out without a pain.

WHEN THE MISTS HAVE CLEARED AWAY.

DARK and dreary days oppress us,
  And the heart seems locked in night;
    But what droppings soon shall bless us;
When we see that heavenly sight!
Oh, if we could pierce the darkness,
  We should see the heavenly day;
We should bask in seas of glory,
  If the mists were cleared away.

No one doubts the sun is shining
  If the sky with clouds is cast;
There must be a silver lining
  When the clouds have onward passed.
Oh, why should we dwell in doubting,
  Or be frightened with dismay?
Glory! we would not cease shouting,
  If the mists were cleared away.

Just beyond, in realms of glory,
  Angels walk the streets of gold;
They rehearse the pleasing story,
  That so often hath been told.
There I see my angel brother,
  Close beside where fountains play;
Oh, my long-lost angel children,
  Now the mists have cleared away.

For one glimpse upon that city
  Will repay a life of pain;
Compensate a world of pity —
  Loved ones lost, but found again!
Oh, dear Saviour, praises to thee!
  Humbly I would watch and pray;
Only waiting to dwell near thee,
  When the mists have cleared away!

MOTHER, HOME, AND HEAVEN.

THREE sweetest names to mortal known,
  Down in this vale of sorrow ;
  We each can claim them for our own,
And sweetest comfort borrow.
The very names are gems of love,
Suggesting strong and perfect love.
Three sweetest names to mortals given,
Are simply, *Mother, Home, and Heaven.*

When sick at heart and tempest-tossed,
  And adverse winds oppress me ;
Oh, when I sink and feel I'm lost,
  These names alone can bless me ;
They lift my feet from miry clay,
And place me in a happy way ;
From this sad heart all fear is driven
In thoughts of Mother, Home, and Heaven.

A stranger in a foreign land,
  Who walks the surging crowd alone,
Can feel how dear is some kind hand,
  Whose pressure makes its friendship known.
Many who thus have sadly felt,
Found comfort as alone they knelt ;
A soothing peace to them is given
In thoughts of Mother, Home, and Heaven.

O precious words, to you I cling,
  And bind you fast forever ;
Sweet happy thoughts to me ye bring,
  Like some sweet, peaceful river ;
Thoughts of a childhood blithe and gay.
When Mother taught her boy to pray,
Though from her side I now am riven,
I think of Mother, Home, and Heaven.

I think of Home, our happy home,
　So modest, yet so fair,
Of loved ones round the old hearth-stone,
　For all were happy there.
We parted from that modest spot,
In other lands to cast our lot.
Though far apart by fortune driven,
Our rest is Mother, Home, and Heaven.

Heaven ! Oh, what a world of bliss
　The very sound brings to the ear.
A precious Home more fair than this,
　From pain and grief, from death and fear,
When weary with the toil of day,
Think thou of rest, and hope and pray ;
Thy sorrows far away are driven,
In thoughts of Mother, Home, and Heaven.

－ － － －

" *IN SPIRIT AND IN TRUTH.* "

GOD ! give me to understand
　The fountain of thy truth ;
　　I wait in patience thy command,
　And seek thee in my youth.
How must I seek thee—how and where ?
　What feeble words can I employ,
To make thee understand my prayer,
　And save thine own, thine erring boy ?

Thy mercy—oh, stupendous love !
　'Tis inexhaustible and free,
And fountains of compassion move,
　Directed by thy majesty.

Do not the great learned men to-day
    But mock thy name, when they define
The only straight and narrow way
    Which each sect claim, is only thine?

One says immersion in the flood
    Is but the only way to Heaven.
Another says, but trust Christ's blood,
    And then no baptism need be given.
One says we need not fear to die,
    When life its course has fully run,
For all are saved in realms on high;
    Salvation is for all, or none.

One says the verdict hath been sealed
    Since time itself began,
And God his plans have all revealed
    To save or damn each man.
One says, the Saviour hath not come
    Another, Christ the Lord is risen,
And all are seeking for a home,
    A freedom from this earthly prison.

O God, my Father, canst thou not see
    Where I am left, so frail and weak?
Which shall I choose, which shall I be?
    Thy counsel I most humbly seek.
My father and my mother lost
    Because we differ in belief!
O God! to me too great the cost,
    Too sad the fate—too deep the grief.

For thou, if no one else, canst see
    The inconsistency I name,
And heaven could not be heaven to me,
    If loved ones suffered in the flame.

THE ENGINEER'S LAST JOURNEY,

Could I be happy over there
  Beyond the narrow bounds of time,
Loved ones in hell, with heaven my share?
  Depart, sad thought, thou art not mine.

This world is beautiful and fair,
  And all seems happy, too, but man,
Forever he seems bowed with care,
  Or with some great religious plan.
Which shall I choose—which shall I claim?
  Oh, teach me, God, thy way to heaven,
Teach me to trust thy holy name,
  Improve this talent thou hast given.

The azure dome of heaven shall be
  The ceiling of my temple fair;
The mountain, valley, plain, or sea
  Shall be my shrine to offer prayer.
The grass and flowers shall sweetly blend,
  To decorate the earthly floor,
From which my humble thanks ascend,
  From which God's mercy I implore.

The thunder cloud, the lightning flash,
  The angry billow, mighty wave,
The tempest that the forests crash,
  Shall be to me God's voice to save,
The rainbow when the storm is o'er,
  The sunbeam when the day is bright,
The soft kiss from the wave to shore,
  The stars of heaven that shine by night,

Shall be the whisperings of God,
  Speaking to me in grandest tone,
And loved ones sleeping 'neath the sod
  Shall tell me he is God alone.

All mankind on this lovely earth
  Shall be my brother—equal—free,
No matter what his name or birth,
  No matter low or high degree.

The Bible, plain, shall be my chart,
  To guide and teach me what I am,
To soothe and pacify my heart,
  And in life's tempest be my calm.
My motto, "Nature," and her work
  All perfect, all divinely fair,
Never a well-known duty shirk,
  And constant fervency in prayer.

MY SUNDAY-SCHOOL SCHOLAR.

THE crimson sunset in the west
  Still lingered in the arms of day,
  A quiet peace, a sober rest
Drove thoughts of care and toil away;
And as the curtains of the night
  Drew closer yet, upon the town,
An angel dressed in snowy white
  From heaven above, to earth came down,—

Came down, a messenger of God,
  To execute his holy will;
How hard it seemed to kiss the rod,
  And bid our troubled hearts be still.
For on the pinions of God's love,
  He bore our darling boy away,
Up to the pure white throne above,
  To sunlight of immortal day.

Ah, doubting heart, far, far away
   Drive all your doubts, and every fear,
How can you doubt ? Why let dismay
   Possess you when the Lord is near.
Short-sighted, erring, as we do,
   How can we tell what is the best ?
God gave, has taken, and he knew
   The weary heart that longed for rest.

How strange, indeed, are all his ways,
   Or else, how blind and dumb are we.
The tumult of the storm he stays,
   Speaks " Peace " unto the troubled sea,
Uses the weak things of this world
   To teach the mighty and the strong,
Untruth from gilded palace hurled,
   And planted truth, against all wrong.

Our darling boy,— ah, precious thought !—
   Our hope, our pride, our darling boy,
What plans for thee our hearts had wrought,
   And we had hoped to reap but joy.
Thy presence never more on earth
   Shall cheer us when the day is done,
As from thy very infant birth
   Thou e'er hast done, our darling son.

But thou art born in heaven again,
   Beyond the bickering blight of time,
Beyond disease and care and pain,
   And joys unspeakable are thine.
·Rest, sweetly rest within the vale,
   Though sad at heart, we will not weep,
We know God's love, it must prevail,
   " He giveth his beloved sleep."

THE RESURRECTION.

THE earth lies wrapped in death,
   All quiet, stark, and cold,
   And frosty winter's chilling breath
Is monarch fierce and bold,
Even the sun has lost its power,
The wind sings dirges, hour by hour,
   And snowy flakes their white unfold.

Scarcely a single sign of life
   In wood, on mountain, or in vale ;
A sepulchre of death, no strife,
   No sad heart-sickening tale.
The elements may war alone,
The earth lies like a monster stone,
   All ghastly, death-like, pale.

Who for one moment now would say
   (Except he knew whereof he spoke)
But what the earth would quiet lay,
   And never have this slumber broke ?
Man could not break that slumber sweet ;
Too weak his hands, too frail his feet,
   His puny arm too weak of stroke.

Frail man would argue, if he dare,
   That thus in death this earth must lie,
" How can it bloom again so fair,
   How can it live—did it not die ?
Such talk is nonsense, foolish, vain ;
It cannot spring to life again,
   I swear by earth and sky."

3

But hark !   The voices of the flowers
　　Are blending sweetly in the earth ;
Their voices strengthen with the hours,
　　They gladly sing in joy and mirth.
The sunshine and the gentle showers
Will soon bring forth the lovely flowers,
　　And we will revel at their birth.

Life ! life ! oh, living, quickening life !
　　The earth is teeming with thy love,
The elements have ceased their strife,
　　The blue sky shines the earth above,
And spring is here—oh, happy thought !
How were such wondrous changes wrought ?
　　Who made earth's wondrous lever move ?

Oh, wondrous change !   Is this the same—
　　The earth—that died six months ago ?
Tell me, O lovely earth, thy name,
　　And tell me, too, what changed thee so !
The earth replied with beaming eye,
" Look not to me, but to the sky,
　　To HIM who doth my secrets know."

And as I toward the heavens gazed,
　　To see what to me should draw near,
As I these eyes by faith upraised,
　　These words distinctly filled my ear ;
" The fullness of the earth is mine,
And while the stars in glory shine,
　　Seed-time and harvest shall appear."

" I am thy Father, fear not thou,
　　But simply trust, all will be well,
Eternal justice clothes my brow ;
　　In life, wherever found, I dwell !
Seek not too far, O finite mind !
Many have sought my power to find
　　The more they seek the less they tell."

And so I bowed my head in shame,
  And sat me down awhile to think,
To ponder on that holy name,
  And at that fountain clear to drink.
Where were my loved ones who had died,
And who in death lay side by side,
  And should they rise or downward sink?

O God! if Thou to life canst bring
  The cold and chilling earth again,
Surely thou canst extract death's sting,
  And conquer sorrow, grief and pain.
I banish doubt, I banish fear,
Harm cannot come if thou be near;
  Under thy wing I would remain.

What must the courts of glory be,
  If earth has such enchanting bliss?
O God! in deep humility
  I trembling hang my hope on this.
Only a few more years of care,
And then a heavenly home to share,
  Where peace, where joy forever is.

FAIR DARBY CREEK.

DARBY Creek, thou art to me
  A pleasant joy forever,
  Though some thy beauty cannot see,
I shall uphold it ever.
Ice-decked with many a shining gem,
  Thy crystal flow is holden;
No plodding boat thy course will stem
  Till sunshine, warm and golden.

The jewels that are shining bright,
  Fringing thy every border,
Are to my mind sweetest delight,
  Arranged in perfect order.
What bride could boast jewels so fair?
  What groom more rich-wrought pleasure!
What king with thee his wealth compare,
  Or count with thee his treasure?

Even the bushes that are near
  Are decked in richest splendor,
As if thou wert to them most dear,
  They humble homage render.
The little snow-bird loves thee too,
  And hops about as merry
As if along thy bank he knew
  Grew many a charming berry.

Beneath thy icy pavement cold
  The little fish are playing
In many a nook, beloved of old,
  Where pearly stones are laying.
Dear little fish! I love you, too;
  So innocent your motion,
That when I stop to think of you
  My thoughts merge to an ocean.

Ocean of wonder, and of love,
  Deep, broad, forever endless,
Watched and protected from above,
  Ye never can be friendless.
Onward, unceasingly ye go,
  Through many a verdant meadow,
When summer's sun is sinking low,
  In sunlight, or in shadow.

The cattle come from many a hill
  To drink pure draughts of pleasure,
Or graze along thy bank at will,
  Resting at perfect leisure.
The sheep drink of thy sparkling wine,
  The young lambs frisk and gambol,
The orb of night on thee doth shine,
  When lovers take a ramble.

Ah, thou hast overheard the vow
  In earnest accents spoken,
And thou hast listened, too, I trow,
  To many a promise broken.
For loving hearts have been the same
  Throughout all time and ages,
And love has been a mystic flame
  On time's unnumbered pages.

The rustic Indian maiden fair
  Hath found her form reflected
In thy pure depths, her dusky hair
  Hath neatly been corrected.
Along thy bank, in twilight hour,
  Where the lovers love to ramble,
Caught by the Cupid mystic power,
  Fearing no bush or bramble.

She for her manly, noble, brave,
  Hath lovingly awaited,
And listened to thy gentle wave,
  Thinking of birds well mated.
The fire from many a wigwam bright
  Hath sent its smoke above thee,
And many hushed from mortal sight
  Once fondly, dearly loved thee.

Back, back unto the setting sun,
　At point of pale-face dagger,
The Indian race compelled to run,
　Or in death's throes to stagger.
No doubt beneath thy gentle wave
　Many a red man entered
The happy hunting-ground so brave,
　On which his rough heart centred.

But now iron girders deftly span
　Thy course in many places,
And snorting steam, controlled by man,
　Brings to thee many faces.
And as they pass in giddy height,
　So rapidly above thee,
I know they look down with delight,
　And say, " Dear creek, I love thee."

THE "NEW VERSION."

I NEVER could have thought it, wife,
　The thing I've heard to-day ;
I'm sorry that in our old life,
　When our few hairs are gray,
That such a thing could happen, dear,
　About the Book of Life,
That we have always loved sincere
　Since you have been my wife.

When you had started off to town
　With our old faithful steed,
As it was early, I laid down
　To rest,— I felt its need,

And as I dozed I heard a rap
  Come sharply from the door,
And I was startled lest mishap
  Had turned you back once more.

So I in haste went to the door
  To find you standing there,
When in a stranger came — he bore
  A volume he called " Prayer."
Well, seeing he was very good,
  I asked him to take a seat,
And warm himself up near the wood,
  Where there was greatest heat.

Well, such a talker I ne'er see
  In all my life before ;
It was not very plain to me
  About the book he bore ;
But when he said " the Bible new,"
  I asked him o'er again,
The old book is the only true,
  And this to me was plain.

Well, then he kind of laughed, and said,
  " You don't keep posted right —
The old book now has long been dead,
  Or hid away from sight.
This is the new revised plan
  Our great men now have given,
To lead progressive, onward man
  Up to the gate of heaven."

Then such a row of papers, too,
  He from his pocket took ;
They all looked very fresh and new,
  Like this " New Version " book.

Well, then he asked me for to read
　　What men like Beecher say,
That hell has passed away, indeed,
　　That hell has passed away.

.

I rubbed my glasses for to see
　　If he had told the truth,
And right before me there it be
　　" New Version — Book of Ruth."
And such a list of names I see,
　　And after each I saw
The letters LL. D., D. D.,
　　He said that meant the law.

Well, well! dear, precious, darling wife,
　　I thought I must have dreamed —
What ? alter that dear Book of Life?
　　Impossible it seemed ;
But there it was as plain as day,
　　" New Version " on each page,
Our Bible dead and passed away,
　　I reckon of old age.

Ten dollars for " New Version," wife,
　　Allow one for the old.
This, God's own book — the word of life,
　　Worth twice its weight in gold ;
And I was awful hurt just then,
　　For he began to write,
And said " all real true gentlemen
　　Bought this new book at sight."

And then I wished for you, dear wife,
　　To come and help me through,
You know by heart this Book of Life,
　　Much better than I do ;

But then he went right on to say,
  Mistakes were in the old,
That these wise men cleared them away,
  And left but purest gold.

I asked him if he never read
  The last words in the book,
And then he lifted up his head,
  And gave me such a look,
And said, " No use for me to try
  To sell to such as you —
Old fossils never, never buy,
  But men of culture do."

Then I arose upon my feet,
  And pointed him the door ;
I heard my heart, so loud it beat,
  I heard him when he swore.
And then he left, I shut the door,
  And opened this dear book,
As often I had done before,
  And of its food partook.

The world has changed, dear, darling wife,
  Since those young days gone by ;
When all enjoyed hope of a life
  Of rest beyond the sky.
There was to us no resting-place,
  Save in this word of truth —
No healing, save the precious grace
  Of God, which sought out youth.

Ah well, our time will soon be o'er,
  Our work will soon be done,
We shall enjoy forevermore,
  The presence of the Son ;
And he will wipe all tears away
  From eyes that fain would weep ;
No sorrow — no more parting day
  When in His arms we sleep.

LINES ON THE DEATH OF KATHARINE LEE
BAYARD.

THE maiden sleeps — sweet be her rest.
    Oh, why should friends and kindred weep ?
  Safe in the city of the blest
God giveth his beloved sleep.
The fairest flowers are first to go,
  God takes the one we love the best ;
And from a world of earthly woe,
  He whispers, " Come and be at rest."

Oh, could we know what bliss is thine,
  Our very hearts would leap with joy ;
The heavenly lights upon thee shine,
  And songs of praise thy lips employ.
She sleeps,— sweet be her calm repose,—
  The idol of a household band,
Trust God, till he his will disclose,
  For he alone can understand.

THOUGHTS ON RECEIVING A PACKAGE OF WED-
DING CAKE.

HERE it lies before me now
   In paper as white as snow,
   With pearly ribbons tied in a bow,
And my thoughts begin to flow.
Oh, wondrous visions do I see
   In that tiny package there,—
That package, prepared so neat for me,
   By one so kind and fair.

A pearly ribbon ! Ah, now I know
   The reason I stop to think,
And why my thoughts begin to flow,
   And tears approach the brink.
For other scenes, not half so fair,
   Have come and gone to me,
And a little head of golden hair
   Methinks I yet can see.

'Twas only a ribbon upon the door
   That the message sadly told,
That our darling Harry the angels bore
   Into the kind shepherd's fold.
But oh, the feelings of the heart,
   Of the grief of a mother that day,
When they made her from her darling part,
   I never could begin to portray.

The sun shone down as fair and bright
   Upon the mourners that day,
But not a heart could see the light,
   For the heart was far away.

But why should we thus in sorrow pine,
  If our darling is safe in the fold ?
Great God ! what mysteries are thine,
  For we left him in the ground so cold.

We humbly bow down at thy feet,
  Poor sin-sick mortals so vile,
And our prayers of mercy we still repeat,
  Still spare us a little while,
Until our humble trust shall be
  As pure and as undefiled
As that of our darling at rest with thee,
  Even our heaven-born child.

At rest ! Oh, wondrous joy indeed !
  We would not call him back,
But in great earnestness proceed
  To follow the Master's track.
Then when our duty here is done,
  And we lay us down to rest
In realms of day, fair as the sun,
  We shall fold him to our breast.

Oh ribbon of pearl on the wedding-cake !
  A lesson thou hast taught,
A leave of thee I now must take ;
  I thank thee for thy thought.
To those who now are man and wife,
  My compliments I pay ;
All through the journey of this life,
  May heaven bless their day.

HOPE.

TO thee, O white-winged dove,
    To thee, O gem of love,
        To thee I fly :
When troubles sore distress,
When comes my loneliness,
        To thee, I cry.

Thy sweet, soft, balmy breath
Gold-tips the pangs of death,
        And sweetly comforts me ;
Oh, whither should I go ?
What power could quell my woe,
        Dear hope, but thee ?

When first I knew the light,
The dawn of reasons bright,
        I then knew thee,
And even then I found
Thy name a pleasant sound,
        Fond hope, to me.

And as I older grew,
Thy name seemed ever new,
        To lift me up ;
For mortal man must know,
That in this vale below,
        Some *bitter* he must sup.

Often in deep despair,
Bowed down with grief and care,
        I droop and pine ;
But, oh thy cheering light
Dispels my darkest night,
        For thou art mine.

I will not let thee go ;
But, while I wait below,
    Shall claim thine aid ;
For if thou fly away—
Ah, tell me—speak and say—
    Shall I not be afraid ?

Thou art my shining star,
Casting thy beams afar,
    Over life's sea ;
And when I fain would sink,
If I thy light may drink,
    I then am free.

And when I come to die,
To thee I then shall fly ;
    Yea, simply trust in thee ;
Knowing that thou wilt keep
And comfort those who weep
    As well as me.

THE DARKTOWN BANQUET.

DE 'possum am a sizzlin' in de fryin' pan ;
    Git out de fiddle an' de bow.
    Happy am de heart ob de hungry colored man ;
    Skip on de heel-tap and de toe.

" Oh, fat am de possum, slick am de coon ;
    Pass dat plate dis way.
We catch 'em prowlin' in de shinin' ob de moon,
    An' day smell like de new-mown hay.

" When I smells de gravy, I can't keep still—
    Where is dat watermillion slice ?
Let de company eat till it gets a fill.
    Ain't dat 'possum gravy nice ?

" De chicken roos' low, de turkey roos' high,
  'Possum climb de old simmon tree,
De little pigs squeal when de darkey cum nigh.
  Yer needn't lock der smoke house for me.

" Oh, some like de yaller gals, some like de black,
  'Coon gravy good enough to-night,
When de music rumbles, make de shanty crack,
  Fling yer feet clear out ob sight."

THE WHIP-POOR-WILL.

WHIP-POOR-WILL in a lonely dell,
  On a moonlight night in May,
  Sat, anxious to hear some lover tell
Of a future, happy day.
A youth and maiden down the lane
  Came slowly, arm in arm,
Singing a song of sweetest strain
  Which acted like a charm.

A rustic seat near by they took,
  While all was calm and still,
But never from them did he look
  This lonely whip-poor-will.
No! not a feather did he shake,
  This queer and strange night-bird,
And not a motion did he make,
  But this is what he heard :—

" When the blossoms in the orchard,
  Come again upon the trees,
Will you marry me, my darling,
  If the Master thus decrees ?

"Will you share my cottage, loved one,
  When the flowers are in bloom,
Be my own forever darling,
  Dissipate my night of gloom?"
Then the bird said, "Whip-poor-will."

Then she hung her head in sadness
  Fondly near him, there to weep.
Suddenly a smile of gladness,
  Then she said, as one in sleep,
"When the roses bloom, my darling,
  I shall rest beneath the flowers,
But my heart I freely give. you;
  Yours—in all life's closing hours."
Then the bird said, "Whip-poor-will."

*   *   *   *   *

When the autumn leaf was falling,
  With its lovely, tinted red,
And the chestnuts brown were falling,
  Lonely lay a maiden—dead.
Near her bier and shroud of whiteness,
  Bowed a young and manly youth,
And the autumn sun in brightness
  Made him realize the truth.

And the flowers followed after,
  Bleak March winds, and April rain.
When the swallows in the rafter
  And returned to us again;
But a sad and lonely creature
  Wandered in that lane, alone,
Every line of face and feature,
  Told that she he loved had gone.

"All my heart is filled with sadness;
  Oh, this anguish of my mind!
But beyond in realms of gladness,
  She in beauty I shall find.

" There in loves embrace forever,
  Paradise shall be our home ;
In its verdant groves forever,
  We forever there, shall roam."
Then the bird said, " Whip-poor-will."

And the whip-poor-will is guarding
  Still that sacred, lonely spot,
And his song as sad as ever
  Proves he never has forgot,
Oh, this earth is full of places
  That are guarded,—guarded still,
For the sake of absent faces,
  By the lone whip-poor-will.
And his song is " Whip-poor-will."

MEMORY.

THE prayer I said when but a boy,
  In dresses, at my mother's knee,
  Whether in sorrow or in joy,
Comes, sweetly comes, to comfort me.
A loving mother's gentle hand
  Then rested gently on my head,
And taught me, made me understand
  How God provided children bread.

Sweet innocence ! And can it be
  That I was once that little boy,—
From every care and sorrow free,
  And nothing knew but brightest joy ?
Wherever in the world I stray,
  Though tempest-tossed with grief and care.
This silver lining's brightest ray
  Shall comfort me—that mother's prayer.

DECORATION DAY.

SWEET flowers cast their fragance sweet,
O day of days, down at thy feet.
   A still voice plainly seems to say,
"Come—this is Decoration Day."
What means this throbbing, surging crowd?
What means this music—singing loud?
A strange enchantment seems to say,
"Come—this is Decoration Day."

The blossoms on a thousand trees
Are filled with music by the bees,
And this is what they seem to say,
"Come—this is Decoration Day."
The rich plumed birds sing very plain:
The gentle spring has come again.
Their very song, so blithe and gay,
Says, "Come—to Decoration Day."

A band of children come along
And sing short snatches of a song.
Now, listen! you will hear them say,
"Come—this is Decoration Day."
Great crowds of women and of men,
Bearing sweet flowers from the glen,
Come surging onward—this—that way;
"Come—this is Decoration Day."

Their song comes to me on the wind:
" Our strife we leave this day behind.
Charity we bring—its folds we lay
On this bright ' Decoration Day.'
The sleeping soldiers, true and brave,
Who died our noble land to save;
The sleeping *Blue*, the sleeping *Gray*,
We honor Decoration Day.

" No more we garner tares—ill-will.
We loved them all, we love them still,
And we repeat what we would say,
' We honor Decoration Day.'
All men may err, when far apart,
Err in their head, if not their heart;
Hence on this morning bright in May
We honor Decoration Day.

" We to their graves will onward trudge,
And God alone shall be our judge.
We trust in him, where'er we stray,
To bless our Decoration Day.
Sweet-loving charity abide
Close to each heart—close to each side,
That we in unity may say,
All hail to Decoration Day.' "

THE METROPOLIS.

ALL the air is filled with sadness,
    Death and terror win the day,
    Nothing fills the heart with gladness
Since the *steamer* sped way.
Who can paint this dreadful picture ?
    Who can tell the awful woe ?
Who can here portray the heart-aches
    Of that night a week ago ?

Men had left behind their loved ones,
    Mothers, fathers, sisters dear,
Sweet-hearts, children, wives and dear ones
    Left at home, for one long year.

Sad the parting, oh, so dreary,
   Sad to bid a last good-bye,
Some went loathful, but t'was hunger
   Drove them from their native sky.

Often had they sought for labor,
   And as often sought in vain,
Wearily they trod back homeward,
   Filled with misery and pain.
Wives and children almost naked,
   Very scanty meat and bread;
Little fire to keep from freezing,
   And a rough and damp straw bed.

Work so scarce, and money scarcer,
   And the "landlord" wants his rent,
With a notice saying harshly,
   " You'll into the street be sent."
Oh the sadness! Oh the sorrow!
   Who can measure heartache's pain,
As it comes, with hungry children,
   And in frenzy sets the brain.

Oh the anguish of the parting!
   Oh the weeping! Oh the tears!
As the monster steamer starting
   Fills the heart with hopes and fears;
Hopes that all may land in safety
   On the distant shore so far,
Fears lest trouble overtake them
   Ere they reach their haven's star.

Brown and sunburnt hands and faces,
   Muscular and sturdy arms
Left our shores for distant places,
   In another land of charms.

Who were saddest of the parties,
   Those who here with us remain,
Or the sturdy bone and muscle
   Who were speeding on the main ?

Why did sleep, that lovely goddess,
   Seem so distant all that night ?
Why such tossing, why such thinking
   Of the loved ones gone from sight ?
Oh, we cannot always answer.
   God hath put in every heart
Something that will make it restless
   When from loved ones far apart.

If the parting was so awful,
   And the last farewell so sad,
What, oh, what could be that anguish
   When the news came fierce and mad :
"All the ship has dashed to pieces,
   Off the North Carolina coast,
Few are saved—if scarcely any ;
   Nearly all on board are lost ! "

Oh the treacherous news that evening,
   That was sped on lightning's breath,
Telling of the great sea steamer,
   Of its loss—of grief and death.
Oh the crying of the women,
   Oh, the grief so sick and sore,
For the loved ones who had perished
   Off the North Carolina shore.

Oh, the orphans and the widows
   Who are left in want and pain ;
For their husbands, for their fathers,
   They shall never see again.
God have mercy on the helpless,
   Bless and comfort in distress,
And we'll try, now and forever
   To ascribe thee rightousness.

FLITTING THOUGHTS.

A S spring revolves with onward flow,
   And sweet birds warble overhead,
   This thought doth sometimes come and go,
" How came the robin's breast so red ?"
Or as in strolling in some lane,
   And seeking flowers fresh and new,
This thought hath come and come again,
   " How came the summer jay so blue ?"

The hand that paints the flowers that grow,
   Who doth the mighty deep enclose,
Has painted the robin's breast just so
   With the same brush he paints the rose.
Yes, he who sends the rain and dew,
   He whom we never should forget,
Painted the jay so very blue ;
   With the same stroke, the violet.

That vast blue scroll, the sky above,
   This mighty Artist painted too.
And flowers, sweet fragments of his love,
   Are scarcely half what he can do.
He paints the heart of man and child,
   And there in strokes of living gold,
He writes, " To me be reconciled,
   I am the Shepherd and the Fold."

BROOKLETS, BIRDS, AND FLOWERS.

USIC of birds—fragrance of flowers—
  Sweet-smelling flowers, greet me to-day !
Murmuring brooklets, chanting the hours,
  Oh, could I read what your sweet voices say.
How very smiling and bright you appear,
  Seeming contented, and happy and free ;
Greeting with pleasure the eye and the ear,
  Singing so sweetly and lovely to me.

Oh, how my heart fills in looking around
  Finding but beauty wherever I gaze ;
Nature so gorgeous, and rich, pleasant sounds.
  Sweet birds chanting melodious praise,
What are you singing, my sweet, pretty bird ?
  Why do you utter such melody sweet ?
Why is your exquisite, cheering song heard,
  The earliest riser with joy to greet ?

"My Maker has filled me with music, you see,
  And I am but praising my Maker,—and friend,
I wish you would join—and try assist me,
  For then all the world will its harmony lend.
I'm trying to do all the good that I can,
  For spring time must end and I fly away.
So that is the reason I warble to man,
  With your kind permission I'll bid you good day."

"What makes you blossom, my sweet pretty flowers?
  Who painted your cheeks so rosy and red ?
And do you intend all the time to be ours,
  To cheer up our pathway as onward we tread ?"
"God gave me my blushes, and gave me my life,
  I blossom on earth but a very short time,
I care nought for wrangling or angry-like strife,
  I'm praising my Maker in music and rhyme.

I soon shall depart to a sunnier clime,
  Where ever I'll bloom with the good and the true;
From sorrow and care, the earth's blighting time,
  I'll go—now bid you a pleasant adieu."

" What are you saying, my sweet noisy brook,
  As over the pebbles you hurriedly go,
Following contentedly, winding and crook, .
  Now running fast, and now running slow?"
" I'm praising my Maker, so good and so kind,
  Who broke off my fetters of ice and of snow,
And that is the reason I carelessly wind,
  I feel so contented and happy, you know.
Bright little children play on my banks,
  And large children too, love to loiter as well.
I ripple forever to heaven my thanks,
  I now must go onward—a happy farewell."

These are the answers, so full and so plain,
  One bright spring morning were whispered to me,
As early I strayed in a green shady lane,
  When nature seemed so happy and free.
And I sat by the brook, 'neath an old oaken tree,
  To wonder and think, and ponder awhile
That nature should be so contented and free,
  And that man and only man, is vile.

CHRISTMAS TIME.

WHITE is the ground with beautiful snow,
  The river is fettered, and hushed its flow.

  Skating and romping, the children at play,
Were never so happy, so merry and gay.

Old Boreas whispers Jack Frost is king;
And Christmas-time comes like a bird on the wing.

The snow-birds are happy in quaintest of dress,
They chirp and are playful, the snow-king they bless.

But hidden away in the old oaken tree,
The squirrel is sleeping as snug as can be.

The rabbit plays gleefully over the snow,
For Christmas and New Year are coming, you know,

Bright on the hearth is the rosy-hued fire,
What more could the heart of mankind desire?

On the table are apples so golden, so red,
Inviting the hungry to partake and be fed.

And the hands of the maid at the organ are fleet
As she plays old December a hasty retreat.

Oh, happy is Christmas, and happy are we
As we look on the children engaged at the tree.

Christ gave to us Christmas, and every good thing
To the heart of humanity still he doth bring.

So while we enjoy this season of bliss,
Remember the power and the glory are his.

CONSISTENCY A JEWEL.

TWO lovers by the river side
  Were whispering softly, as the tide
    Came gently near the shore,
And in the deepening twilight there
They vowed their future lots to share
    Forever, evermore.

"I pledge by all the stars above,
  You are my first, my only love,
    I want none else but thee;
By yonder 'dipper' in the sky,
For *thee* I live, for *thee* I die.
    Thou art the world to me."

Said she, "I pledge by yonder moon,
Through sunshine, and through midnight gloom,
    To *thee*—my only one;
I pledge thee further by this tide,
By thee I ever shall abide,
    Till life itself is done."

Look at that *golden dipper*—see
It hanging in rich mystery,
    A beauty to behold!
It changes never,—and I say
Man's love must be the self-same way—
    It never can grow old.

See yonder moon—Lo! it has gone,
No traces can I look upon;
    Now, let us view the tide:
It too has *changed*—how sad to tell!
Does woman's love do so, as well?
    And has my true love's died?

THE ABSENT ONE.

A S we gather at the fireside,
　　When the busy day is done,
　　And we count our darlings over,
　How we miss the absent one!
And our very hearts are stricken
　When we view the vacant chair,
For our lovely little darling
　Seemed so bright and happy there.

Then the thought, "Where is our loved one?"
　Flashes through the brain and mind,
"Safe in Heaven," comes the answer.
　"Seek, and you shall surely find!
Ye shall meet your little children
　In the flowery fields of light,
Jesus loved your little darlings,
　And they rest in sweet delight."

How we miss them in the spring-time,
　When the flowers bloom so bright,
For the music of their laughter
　Filled our hearts with pure delight.
They are safe with God in heaven,
　Though we left them at the tomb,
In the paradise of glory,
　Where the flowers forever bloom.

CHRISTMAS.

'TIS midnight! Darkness covers the earth! Behold the star resting over the manger! Listen to the cry of the infant Savior! Faint though it be, that cry comes thundering down the ages with increased force, until the world halts to listen! Behold the shepherds searching for the Babe! See them rejoice!

The night wears away, and behold, the day breaketh! See the faint glimmer of light, barely discernible in the East! The earth is as a dungeon, but wait! The light grows brighter, until the curtains of morning are opened, and pinned back by diamonds of richest ray! * * * 'Tis morning! The darkness has been chased away, and hill and vale are illumined with the full effulgence of the god of day, as he marches across the heavens like a mighty giant. As with the physical kingdom — things seen by mortal eyes — so with the spiritual kingdom of Christ, as seen by the eyes of faith! As the darkness is driven back by the sun, so the Son of God drives superstition, heresy, and schism away, and fills their places with that "love that passeth understanding," with that "peace that floweth like a river." The sun carries health and happiness to mankind, so the Son of Righteousness riseth with healing in his wings, permeating even to the heart of the sinner and the unconverted, and diffusing the glorious light of Liberty! Blessed Christmas; hallowed Birthday! May each succeeding one find us a year nearer heaven, a year nearer the crown reserved for the followers of that dear Savior who was lifted up that He might draw all mankind unto himself!